STELLA: THE DOG WITH THE BIG HEART

BY THEA FELDMAN ★ ILLUSTRATED BY CHRIS DANGER

Ready-to-Read

Simon Spotlight

New York   London   Toronto   Sydney   New Delhi

SIMON SPOTLIGHT
An imprint of Simon & Schuster Children's Publishing Division
1230 Avenue of the Americas, New York, New York 10020
This Simon Spotlight edition July 2015
For information about special discounts for bulk purchases, please contact Simon & Schuster Special Sales at
1-866-506-1949 or business@simonandschuster.com.
The Simon & Schuster Speakers Bureau can bring authors to your live event. For more information or to book
an event contact the Simon & Schuster Speakers Bureau at 1-866-248-3049 or visit our website at
www.simonspeakers.com.
Manufactured in the United States of America 1023 LAK
2 4 6 8 10 9 7 5 3
Library of Congress Cataloging-in-Publication Data
Feldman, Thea, author.
Stella : the dog with the big heart / by Thea Feldman ; illustrated by
Chris Danger.
pages cm. — (Hero dog)
Summary: "Stella is a real dog. She is a special dog with an important
job. Stella is a therapy dog and she creates happiness wherever she goes.
That makes her a hero to many people. Read her story to find out more about
Stella and what makes her a hero dog."— Provided by publisher.
Audience: Ages 5–7.
Audience: K to grade 3.
Includes bibliographical references and index.
ISBN 978-1-4814-2243-7 (pbk. : alk. paper) — ISBN 978-1-4814-2244-4
(hardcover : alk. paper) — ISBN 978-1-4814-2245-1 (eBook)
1.Dogs—Therapeutic use—Juvenile literature. 2. Working dogs—Juvenile
literature. I. Danger, Chris, illustrator. II. Title.
RM931.D63F45 2015
615.8'5158—dc23
2014030115

Stella jumps onto a man's lap.
The man is in a wheelchair.
He cannot walk.
It is hard for him to speak.
But when Stella sits in his lap,
he speaks with his smile.

The man lives in a place
where people take care of others
who have special health needs.

Why is Stella there?
Stella is a therapy dog.
She and her owner, Marissa,
visit people who have health issues.
Stella makes people happy,
just by being Stella.

"Is Stella soft?"
a nurse asks the man.
"Yes!" he says, speaking slowly.
The man answers
more questions about Stella.
He strokes her fur.
Stella licks him.

Stella gets off the man's lap.
She and Marissa start to leave
the room.
The man begins to cry!

Stella comes back right away.
She climbs up into the man's lap.
He stops crying.
He hugs Stella.
He smiles again.

He even gives Stella a kiss!

Stella loves visiting the man.
She loves being a therapy dog.
Stella went to a special school
to become a therapy dog.

Therapy dog school is hard.
A dog has to pass a lot of tests!
Stella had to show she was friendly.

She had to show she understands
different commands, like "Sit!"
and "Heel!"

Stella had to show she doesn't mind
being around a lot of people
at once.

She had to show she doesn't mind
being around crutches
or wheelchairs.
Not every dog can pass all the tests.
Not every dog can be a therapy dog.

To become a therapy dog,
Stella had to be able to obey orders.
She had to refuse treats
offered to her.
She had to ignore food on the floor.
Not every dog can do that,
but Stella can!

Stella visits many people
who cannot walk or
who have trouble walking.
One woman usually uses a
wheelchair.
When Stella comes to see her,
the woman gets up and uses a walker.

She holds on to the walker.
She holds on to Stella's leash, too.
The woman moves slowly,
but Stella doesn't mind.
Stella likes taking a walk
with her new friend!

Stella visits many people
who cannot move their bodies
on their own.
With the help of a nurse,
one young man strokes Stella's fur.
The man's eyes get wide,
and then he smiles broadly.
Stella is happy too!

Stella also visits older people
who live in nursing homes.
They laugh when they see Stella.
They lean down to pat her curly fur.
They take turns hugging Stella.
Stella wags her tail.
She loves it!

Stella also visits children
who are sick.
Some of them have serious
illnesses.
It can be a very scary time.
But not when Stella stops by!

STELLA

When Stella comes to visit,
the children forget
that they are sick
for a little while.
They play with Stella.
They even draw pictures of Stella!

It doesn't matter to Stella
if people can walk or talk.
Or if they are sick.

And it doesn't matter to her
if they are young or old.
Stella loves everyone.

Stella has a huge heart.
She also has a huge wardrobe!
Stella has a blue, flowered dress.
She has a purple dress with
white polka dots too.

One reason everyone loves it when Stella visits is that they can't wait to see if she's wearing a new outfit!

In just one year,
Stella visited places as a
therapy dog more than 500 times!
That earned her the highest title
for a therapy dog from her school.

And that's not all!
Not long after, Stella was chosen
as the winner in the Therapy Dog
category at the American Humane
Association Hero Dog Awards.
Congratulations, Stella!

As a therapy dog,
Stella makes people happy.
She helps them forget their troubles.
That has been true for Marissa
since the day she met Stella.
Before Stella came into her life,
Marissa was going through a hard time.

Marissa met Stella when
Stella was just four months old.
Stella sat on Marissa's lap.
She licked Marissa's face.
She showed Marissa love.

Marissa loved Stella right back.
It was impossible not to!

Stella made Marissa smile again. She made Marissa very happy. Marissa decided she needed to share Stella with other people and make them happy too.

That's how Stella became
a therapy dog and a hero
to everyone she knows.
Because of all she does,
most people who meet Stella
think of her as a miracle with fur!